SHANE
the Lone Ethnographer

SHANE
THE LONE ETHNOGRAPHER

A BEGINNER'S
GUIDE TO
ETHNOGRAPHY

by:
SALLY
CAMPBELL
GALMAN

AltaMira
PRESS

A Division of
ROWMAN & LITTLEFIELD PUBLISHERS, INC.
Lanham • New York • Toronto • Plymouth, UK

AʟᴛᴀMɪʀᴀ Pʀᴇss
A division of Rowman & Littlefield Publishers, Inc.
A wholly owned subsidiary of The Rowman & Littlefield Publishing Group, Inc.
4501 Forbes Boulevard, Suite 200
Lanham, MD 20706
www.altamirapress.com

Estover Road
Plymouth PL6 7PY
United Kingdom

British Library Cataloguing in Publication Information Available

Library of Congress Cataloguing-in-Publication Data

Galman, Sally Campbell.
    Shane, the lone ethnographer : a beginner's guide to ethnography / written and
  Illustrated by Sally Campbell Galman.
      p.   cm.
    Includes bibliographic references.
    ISBN-13: 978-0-7591-0344-3 (pbk. : alk. paper)
    ISBN-10: 0-7591-0344-5 (pbk. : alk. paper)
    1. Ethnology—Research. 2. Ethnology—Field work. 3. Ethnology—Methodology. I.
Title.

  GN345.G35 2007
  305.800772—dc22   2006052637

Printed in the United States of America

⊗™ The paper used in this publication meets the minimum requirements of American
National Standard for Information Sciences—Permanence of Paper for Printed Library
Materials, ANSI/NISO Z39.48–1992.

CONTENTS

SPECIAL THANKS TO:

ALL THE FOLKS AT THE UNIVERSITY OF COLORADO SCHOOL OF EDUCATION — ESPECIALLY MARGARET LECOMPTE AND MARGARET EISENHART — WHO TAUGHT ME ABOUT ETHNOGRAPHY... AND THEN SOME.

MY FRIENDS, WHO HELPED SO MUCH — ESPECIALLY ERIC EITELJORG, WHO PROVIDED INSPIRATION AND HILARITY FROM THE BEGINNING.

MITCH ALLEN, DAN LISTON & NANCY VANDEVENDER, WHO HAD FAITH IN MY LITTLE DRAWINGS.

AND:

MY BROTHER,   MY HUSBAND

& MY PARENTS, WHO GAVE ME LOVE, ENCOURAGEMENT AND LOTS AND LOTS OF ART SUPPLIES.

SCL

SHANE, THE LONE ETHNOGRAPHER!

A BEGINNER'S GUIDE TO ETHNOGRAPHY

written and illustrated by
Sally Campbell Galman

A LONE ON THE RANGE

"A FISTFUL OF RESERVE READING"

MEET SHANE.

A GRADUATE STUDENT...

WESTERN BUFF...

PROCRASTINATOR...

...AND NOVICE RESEARCHER.

INDEED, IT IS THAT TIME IN HER GRADUATE COURSEWORK WHEN OUR INTREPID HEROINE MUST PAIR HER VAST KNOWLEDGE OF THEORY WITH WORKIN RESEARCH METHODS. SO, WE FIND SHANE SITTING IN CLASS...

IT IS ALSO WORTH NOTING THAT SHE RUNS A BIT ON THE IMAGINATIVE SIDE...

...IF NOT ALWAYS ON TOPIC.

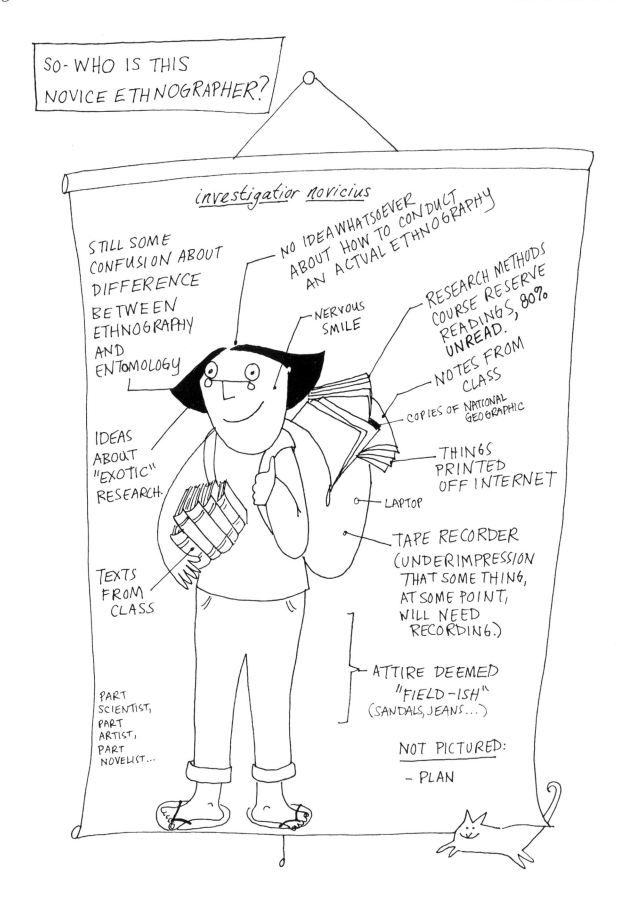

HI EVERYONE! C'MON IN!

ETHNOGRAPHIC STUDIES ARE NOT RECREATED IN LABORATORY SETTINGS

INSTEAD OF THE PEOPLE COMING TO YOU -- YOU GO TO THEM - TO THEIR NATURAL SETTINGS.

HENCE, "NATURALISTIC."

YOU HANG OUT IN THE ENVIRONMENT OF THAT COMMUNITY. SO, IF YOU STUDY A GROUP OF HOTEL MAIDS...

I'M AT THE HILTON ALL DAY!

YOU GOT IT!

BUT -- WAIT → I THOUGHT THIS WAS RESEARCH.

IT IS!

SO, WHERE ARE ALL THE WHITE LAB COATS? THE BEEPING EQUIPMENT?

sigh...

THAT'S ONLY ONE WAY OF DOING RESEARCH - ONLY ONE WAY OF LOOKING AT THE WORLD!

WE TALKED ABOUT CULTURE AND THE NATURALISTIC STUDY - BUT LET'S TALK ABOUT RESEARCH PARADIGMS

PARADIGMS ARE WAYS RESEARCHERS APPROACH THEIR WORK - HOW THEY ASK QUESTIONS, HOW THEY GET ANSWERS, AND WHO HAS THE ANSWERS THEY NEED!

ONE OF THE PARADIGMS IS WHAT YOU ARE THINKING ABOUT - LAB SETTINGS AND STUFF LIKE THAT ARE SOMETIMES PART OF POSITIVISTIC, OR OBJECTIVE - QUANTITATIVE RESEARCH.

WHILE OTHER RESEARCHERS' WORK MAY BE MORE INTERPRETIVE - QUALITATIVE, OR EVEN CRITICAL - THEORETICAL.

WHAT - WAIT - YOU'RE GOING TOO FAST.

WAIT - HOLD ON AND JUST LISTEN.

SO - THERE ARE A COUPLE OF WAYS TO CONDUCT RESEARCH -

IN EDUCATIONAL RESEARCH IN PARTICULAR, THIS CONFLICT CAME TO A HEAD DURING THE 1980's - IT WAS CALLED THE "PARADIGM WARS" IN RESEARCH ON TEACHING. THE POSITIVISTS AND INTERPRETIVISTS WOULD DUKE IT OUT!

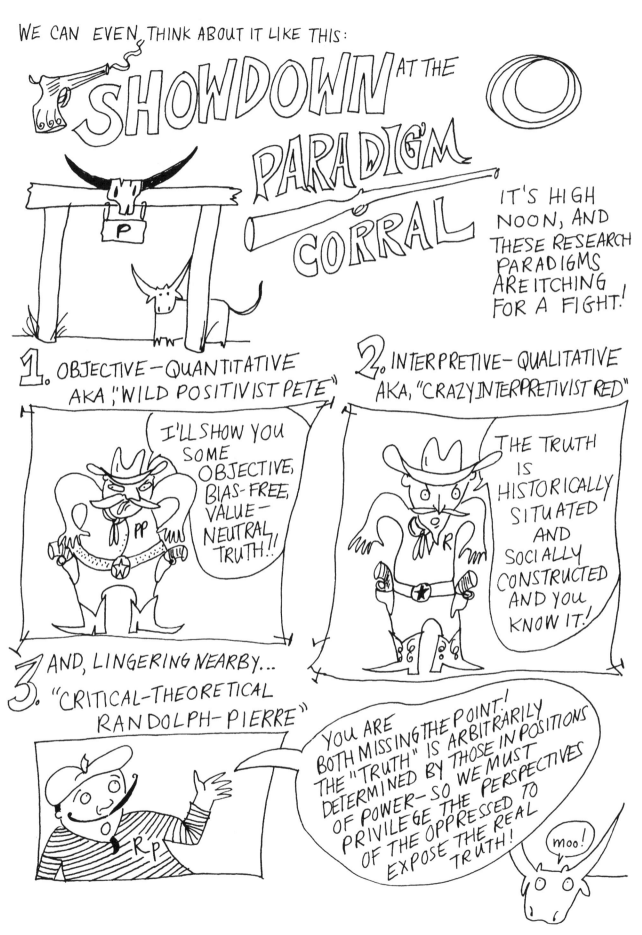

NOW, THE VARIOUS ISSUES AT THE RANCH ARE OF A TROUBLING NATURE...

AN ETHNOGRAPHIC APPROACH HAS BEEN DEEMED THE BEST WAY TO GET AN IDEA — AFTER ALL, ETHNOGRAPHY IS A GOOD WAY TO DO ALL THIS:

WELL, THERE'S ONLY ONE UDDER DOWN HERE—

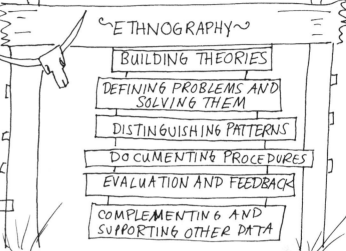

~ETHNOGRAPHY~

BUILDING THEORIES

DEFINING PROBLEMS AND SOLVING THEM

DISTINGUISHING PATTERNS

DOCUMENTING PROCEDURES

EVALUATION AND FEEDBACK

COMPLEMENTING AND SUPPORTING OTHER DATA

THEY'RE ALL ETHNOGRAPHERS, BUT THEIR PARADIGMS SUGGEST DIFFERENT WAYS OF DOING ALL THESE THINGS.

1. POSITIVIST PETE, WHOSE PARADIGM SUGGESTS A NEUTRAL, OBJECTIVE SUBJECT AND A NEUTRAL, OBJECTIVE, BIAS-FREE RESEARCHER, WORKS ON DEVELOPING GENERALIZABLE RULES OF CAUSATION.

2. INTERPRETIVIST RED IS INVOLVED WITH PARTICIPANTS ELICITING MEANINGS FROM INVOLVED, SUBJECTIVE PARTICIPANTS TO CREATE SHARED UNDERSTANDINGS.

NOW, CLEM, I...

SO CLEM, TELL ME MORE ABOUT THIS WHOLE THING WHAT MEANS TO YOU.

I FEEL LIKE...

THE SUBJECT IS ENGAGED IN RITUALIZED SPEECH WITH THE OTHERS — THIS SPEECH IS THIER WAY OF SHOWING COMRADESHIP IN THIS CULTURE...

HE IS* "OBJECTIVE" AND DOES HIS OBSERVATION FROM A DISTANCE. IT'S ALL ABOUT THE RESEARCHER.
(* = OR, RATHER, HE CLAIMS TO BE...)

FOR RED, IT'S ALL ABOUT THE SUBJECT — HIS IDEAS. RED IS A PARTICIPANT OBSERVER; SO, HE DOES HIS OBSERVATION WHILE PARTICIPATING WITH THE SUBJECTS.

WHERE'S THE CRITICAL GUY?

WAIT!

Remember -- the belief that other cultures were less developed or inferior to some, particularly the European cultures, was an accepted hierarchy then.

SO, I SHOULD ADD THOSE TO MY LIST. ETHNOGRAPHY—A TOOL OF ANTHROPOLOGY—① USES LOTS OF DATA SOURCES,

② and should be culturally relativistic. Right.

AND SHOULD ③ TAKE PLACE IN NATURALISTIC SETTINGS, ④ USE CULTURE AS A LENS FOR UNDERSTANDING, ⑤ BE ABOUT THE CULTURAL AND SOCIAL LIFE OF COMMUNITIES, ⑥ BE DESCRIPTIVE IN NATURE AND...

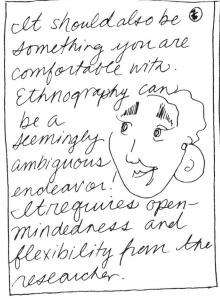

It should also be ⑦ something you are comfortable with. Ethnography can be a seemingly ambiguous endeavor! It requires open-mindedness and flexibility from the researcher.

SO, IF I WERE A PAINFULLY SHY, INFLEXIBLE, ARROGANT PERSON WHO DOESN'T LIKE TO LEAVE MY HOUSE, GET MY HANDS DIRTY OR DEAL WITH HUMAN BEINGS OR AMBIGUITY...

IT'S NOT FOR ME!

You've got it.

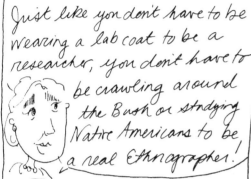

Later at Shane's apartment...

Chapter Three

The Good, The Bad & The BEGINNER!

or

"Yes, you *are* getting ahead of yourself."

"GOOD STUDY, BAD STUDY"

WINNERS FINISH THEIR STUDIES; LOSERS GO SLOWLY INSANE PLAYING THE COROLLARY GAME, "WHAT WAS I THINKING?!?"

1. Step one: HAVE YOU DEFINED YOUR RESEARCH QUESTION OR THE RESEARCH PROBLEM YOU WISH TO EXAMINE? YEP!

2. STEP TWO: HAVE YOU EVALUATED THE APPROPRIATENESS OF ETHNOGRAPHY AS A WAY TO APPROACH THE QUESTION? YEP!

3. Step Three: HAVE YOU COME UP WITH A PLAN, OR A Research Design? NO? WELL...

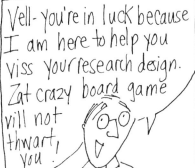

SO LET'S GET THIS STRAIGHT—

YOU'VE BEEN GETTING A TAN IN THE TROPICS, TALKING TO TROBRIAND ISLANDERS—

JA...

HOW IS THAT REMOTELY LIKE MY STUDY OF SOME ACADEMICS?!

HOLD ZE HORSES! WHY EEZ IT DIFFERENT? CULTURES AND CONTEXTS VARY, BUT CULTURE IS PRESENT EVEN IF IT IS FAMILIAR!

In my work on social and cultural institutions, there are lots of things that apply to all kinds of sites!

Including ze Academic context...

HALLOWED HALLS OF HIGHER LEARNING

OKAY...

Now— I want you to start thinking about your study population and site. You've worked hard to think of a compelling problem and isolate your method— ethnography— Now there are three concepts from my work that I want you to think about...

1. SOCIAL BEHAVIOR CAN BE UNDERSTOOD IN TERMS OF INDIVIDUALS' MOTIVATIONS ROOTED IN BOTH "RATIONAL" AS WELL AS "MAGICAL" THINKING... SCIENTIFICALLY "VALIDATED" THOUGHT AND RELIGIOUS, RITUAL OR SO-CALLED "IRRATIONAL" THOUGHT.

2. DIFFERENT PARTS OF A CULTURE INTERCONNECT TO MAKE SYSTEMS THAT INDIVIDUALS USE TO COPE WITH CIRCUMSTANCES

3. THE BEST WAY TO UNDERSTAND THOSE SYSTEMS IS TO LOOK AT THE LITTLE PARTS IN TERMS OF THE EVIDENT FUNCTION.

★ YOU CAN DO ETHNOGRAPHIES WITH VERY SMALL GROUPS — EVEN ONE OR TWO PARTICIPANTS!

Yes-ask. Subject wrangling can get tricky.

WRANGLING? YEAH... LIKE AT THE RODEO...

Kind of — but without the ropes and the violence. Think of the people you study as participants — that may help.

AH - BUT A RODEO!

I IMAGINE MY POTENTIAL PARTICIPANTS RANGING FREE, IN THEIR NATURAL SETTING.

IF IT'S GRANTED, I'M IN BUSINESS. BUT...

... AND I ENLIST THEM! (BUT, I ASK PERMISSION BEFORE I LASSO THEM...)

IF THE GROUP IS SMALL, I NEED TO BE SURE TO GET ALL OF THEM — OTHERWISE I COULD MISS KEY MEMBERS

IF THE GROUP IS VERY BIG, I NEED TO THINK ABOUT WHETHER OR NOT I HAVE THE CAPACITY TO HANDLE A LARGE POPULATION

For the purposes of your descriptive ethnography, you are interested in the typical group member of the group — things in common, etc.

ZO - you get permission and zen get to ze library!

LIBRARY?

Yep. You have some theory to read! See you later, Lone Ethnographer...

sigh...

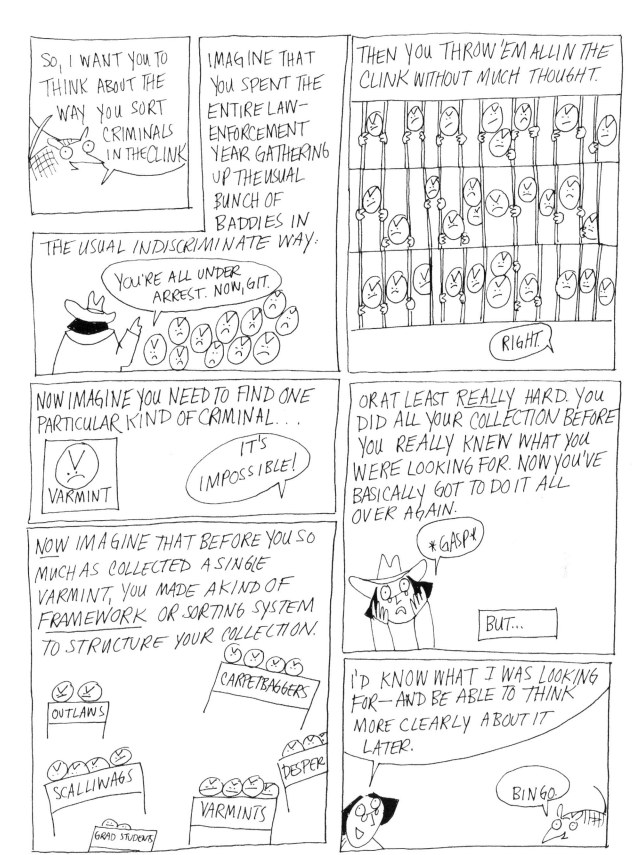

SO, WHILE WE WAIT FOR SHANE, LET'S TAKE A SHORT-CUT...

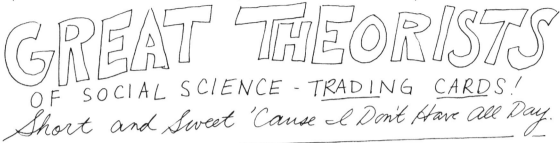

GREAT THEORISTS

OF SOCIAL SCIENCE - TRADING CARDS!

Short and Sweet 'Cause I Don't Have All Day.

COLLECT 'EM ALL! THE ULTIMATE SOCIAL SCIENCE GEEK ACCESSORY AND COLLECTOR'S ITEM!

MARGARET MEAD

INVESTIGATED CULTURE IN SAMOA IN <u>COMING OF AGE IN SAMOA</u> (1949)

THIS WAS CONSIDERED A GROUNDBREAKING WORK IN NORMS FOR INTERACTIONS BETWEEN AND AMONG THE SEXES — AND HOW THE WESTERN MODEL IS NOT UNIVERSAL.

PIERRE BOURDIEU

COINED THE TERM <u>HABITUS</u> TO DESCRIBE WHAT PEOPLE

TAKE FOR GRANTED FROM OUR EARLY SOCIALIZATION AS A POST-STRUCTURALIST, HE CLAIMED THAT STRUCTURE WAS IN PART A HUMAN CREATION, HOWEVER UNCONSCIOUS.

MY ADVISOR

PASTE PHOTO HERE

LIST ACCOLADES HERE

EMILE DURKHEIM

FOCUSE ON EXAMINING SOCIAL AND CULTURAL HAPPENINGS AS THEY <u>FUNCTION</u> TO MAINTAIN SOCIAL STRUCTURE. HENCE, THE SCHOOL OF ANTHROPOLOGY THINKING KNOWN AS FUNCTIONALISM.

CLIFFORD GEERTZ

SYMBOLIC ANTHROPOLOGY: HOW SYMBOLS OPERATE WITHIN CULTURES FOR INDIVIDUAL USE. CULTURE IS, AFTER ALL, A SOCIAL PHENOMENON, BEST VIEWED FROM AN INTERPRETIVE, NOT EXPERIMENTAL STANCE. THE POINT OF ETHNOGRAPHY IS TO DECIPHER THE HIERARCHY OF SOCIAL STRATA.

COLLECT 'EM ALL!

GEORGE H. MEAD

FOUNDER OF SOCIAL PSYCHOLOGY, SOCIOLOGIST MEAD FOCUSED ON THE INDIVIDUAL EXPERIENCE AS STUDIED IN THE SOCIAL CONTEXT- AND INEXTRICABLY SITUATED THEREIN. MANY OF HIS WORKS WERE WRITTEN POSTHUMOUSLY BY STUDENTS. FOUNDER OF THE CHICAGO SCHOOL OF INTERACTIONISM.

CLAUDE LEVI-STRAUSS

THE "FATHER" OF STRUCTURALISM WAS INTERESTED IN SOCIAL ORGANIZATION, & APPLIED MODELS FROM STRUCTURAL LINGUISTICS TO THE STUDY OF CULTURE, SUGGESTING THAT THE STRUCTURE OF HUMAN THOUGHT PROCESSES IS THE SAME ACROSS CULTURES.

RUTH BENEDICT

WROTE ABOUT THE JAPANESE AND "NATIONAL CHARACTER" IN THE CHRYSANTHEMUM AND THE SWORD. CO-FOUNDER OF THE CONFIGURATIONAL APPROACH: CULTURES ARE MADE UP OF MEMBERS' SIMILAR BELIEFS & IDEAS.

FRANZ BOAS

CHANGED THE STRUCTURE OF ANTHROPOLOGY FROM A COLONIALIST, HIERARCHICAL EVOLUTIONARY VIEW TO ONE THAT ASSUMES EQUALITY OF CULTURES & INDIVIDUALS. SO, NO MORE ASSESSMENTS OF "PRIMITIVE." DEFINED CULTURE AS IT IS USED IN MODERN ANTHROPOLOGY IN WORK WITH NATIVE AMERICANS.

BRONISLAW MALINOWSKI

UNDERSTOOD BEHAVIOR IN TERMS OF INDIVIDUALS' MOTIVATIONS—BOTH "RATIONAL" AND "MAGICAL", WITH A FOCUS ON THE INTER-CONNECTEDNESS OF ELEMENTS IN A CULTURAL GROUP AND THE ORGANIC NEEDS OF HUMAN BEINGS. HIS WORK WITH THE TROBRIAND ISLANDERS WAS EXTENSIVE.

A. R. RADCLIFFE-BROWN

FOUNDER OF STRUCTURAL-FUNCTIONALISM, FOCUSED ON SOCIAL STRUCTURE AND SYSTEMS OF RELATIONSHIPS. CONSIDERED INDIVIDUALS IRRELEVANT AND REPLACEABLE IN THE LARGER SOCIAL STRUCTURE, WHICH HAD PRIMACY. ALONG WITH MALINOWSKI, HE PUSHED FOR A PARADIGM SHIFT.

EDWARD SAPIR

LINGUISTIC ANTHROPOLOGY AND AMERINDIAN LANGUAGE, ALONG WITH HEAVY INFLUENCE FROM THE WRITINGS OF JUNG LED HIM TO BEGIN WORK WITH CULTURE, PERSONALITY AND THE INDIVIDUAL IN ANTHROPOLOGY.

E.E. EVANS-PRITCHARD

WROTE THE FIRST PROFESSIONAL ETHNOGRAPHY OF AN AFRICAN PEOPLE. WORKED WITH CONCEPTS OF KINSHIP WHICH WOULD SHAPE POLITICAL THEORY. SAW SOCIAL ANTH. AS "COMPARATIVE HISTORY" - NOT SCIENCE.

LUCY MAIR

DID FIELDWORK ON SOCIAL CHANGE IN UGANDA. AT THE FOREFRONT OF APPLIED ANTHROPOLOGY, SHE WAS DEEPLY CONCERNED ABOUT COLONIAL PRACTICES IN A AFRICA, WRITING <u>NATIVE POLICIES IN AFRICA</u> AND <u>ANTHROPOLOGY AND SOCIAL CHANGE</u>.

VICTOR TURNER

WORKED IN SYMBOLIC ANTHROPOLOGY, SAW SYMBOLS AS OPERATING VARIABLES WITH SHARED MEANINGS THAT TIE INDIVIDUALS TO THE SOCIAL GROUP. STUDIED THE NDEMBU IN AFRICA, DEVELOPED THE CONCEPT OF THE "SOCIAL DRAMA."

NOW YOU KNOW WHAT YOU'RE INTERESTED IN FINDING OUT, THE WAY IN WHICH YOU WILL FIND THINGS OUT (ETHNOGRAPHY) AND THE THEORETICAL FRAMEWORK YOU'LL USE TO STRUCTURE YOUR THINKING. SO, IT'S TIME TO READ THE WORK OF OTHERS TO SEE WHAT THEY'VE FOUND OUT ABOUT THIS TOPIC IN THEIR STUDIES. THIS TASK IS COMMONLY KNOWN AS THE:

"Desperado"

SCHMALTZY LOVE SONG OR MNEMONIC DEVICE
— you choose —

Why *DON'T* YOU come to your senses?

DIG INTO OLD COURSE PACKETS, TALK TO PROFESSORS AND OTHER STUDENTS TO IDENTIFY KEY STUDIES TO BEGIN WITH.

END: GO TO THE END OF AN ARTICLE TO SEE WHAT IS IN THE BIBLIOGRAPHY, AS WELL AS ANYTHING IN THE ENDNOTES.

SO WHAT? REMEMBER THIS IS A CRITICAL REVIEW. AS YOU READ AND THINK ASK YOURSELF QUESTIONS ABOUT THE LITERATURE AND WHERE YOUR WORK MIGHT FIT IN.

PEER REVIEWED: HAVE YOUR SOURCES COME FROM A SOURCE THAT IS SUBJECT TO PEER REVIEW?

ELECTRONIC SOURCES: SOME GREAT DATABASES ARE OUT THERE BUT THINGS CAN GET TRICKY — LEARN TO TELL GOOD STUFF FROM INTERNET SLUSH.

RECENT: BOOKS ARE OKAY AND JOURNALS ARE BETTER. STAY UP-TO-DATE.

ANNOTATED BIBLIOGRAPHIES ARE DIFFERENT FROM A LIT REVIEW: DON'T SUM UP ARTICLE BY ARTICLE. RATHER, FOCUS ON THEMES.

DEVELOP: A GOOD REVIEW WILL HELP YOU REFINE AND DEVELOP YOUR RESEARCH QUESTIONS.

ORGANIZE YOUR REVIEW INTO CATEGORIES LIKE WHAT'S IN YOUR THEORETICAL FRAMEWORK.

Chapter Five

IRB

FROM THE PEOPLE
WHO BROUGHT YOU
THE IRS

PAPER WORK

★ ANIMALS HAVE RIGHTS, TOO. THEY HAVE *THEIR OWN PROTECTIONS AT MANY RESEARCH INSTITUTIONS.*

WHILE IRB'S—INSTITUTIONAL REVIEW BOARDS—EXIST TO PROTECT ALL HUMAN SUBJECTS, MANY PEOPLE ABUSED IN "SCIENTIFIC" STUDIES WERE MORE VULNERABLE THAN OTHERS.

IRB

TUSKEGEE PUBLIC HEALTH SERVICE

SUBJECTS WHO CANNOT READ, DEVELOPMENTALLY DISABLED PERSONS, PRISONERS, CHILDREN OR MEMBERS OF OTHERWISE MARGINALIZED GROUPS ARE VULNERABLE TO

U.S. HUMAN RADIATION EXPERIMENTS

BEING FORCED, COERCED OR TRICKED.

WHEN THIS ABUSE CAME TO LIGHT AT NUREMBERG AND OTHER INSTANCES, PROTECTIVE DOCUMENTS WERE DRAFTED.

THE NUREMBERG CODE (1947)

DECLARATION OF HELSINKI (1964)

THE BELMONT REPORT (1979)

ALL THREE FOCUS ON THE SAME THEMES:

all Research must Exhibit:

1. RESPECT

ALL INDIVIDUALS' DIGNITY AND AUTONOMY AND OFFER SPECIAL PROTECTION FOR THOSE WITH VULNERABILITY.

2. BENEFICENCE:

MINIMIZE HARM, MAXIMIZE BENEFITS TO SUBJECTS.

3. JUSTICE:

BE FAIR IN HOW YOU DISTRIBUTE BENEFITS AND RISKS.

YOU MUST INCLUDE A STANDARD INFORMED CONSENT FORM—

DO YOU CONSENT FREELY TO GET WRANGLED IN THIS HERE RING?

AH SHOR DO.

MAKING SPECIAL PROVISIONS FOR VULNERABLE SUBJECTS.

SO, LIKE, I'M GOING TO STUDY SOME ILLEGAL IMMIGRANT, HOMELESS, EX-CON, NON-ENGLISH SPEAKING PREGNANT TEEN PROSTITUTES WHO SHOOT SMACK AND ARE IN A GANG. IS THAT, LIKE, A PROBLEM?

AND MAKING WAYS TO PROTECT ALL SUBJECTS' PRIVACY.

YOUR PSEUDONYM... YOU'VE CHOSEN "PRISCILLA"?

BE SURE TO ALSO ATTACH ALL SUPPORTING DOCUMENTS, LIKE LETTERS OR QUESTIONNAIRES.

OW.

AND THEN IT GOES TO THE IRB COMMITTEE!

WE ONLY LOOK LIKE DRIED UP OLD ACADEMIC HUSKS BENT ON YOUR DOOM— BUT WE'RE NOT.

WE'RE REALLY VERY NICE.

AND YOU'RE READY TO GO!

WIN

Chapter 5½

WAIT A SEC— BEFORE YOU EVEN THINK ABOUT COLLECTING ANY DATA... YOU NEED SOME QUICK TIPS ABOUT THE FIELD!

STOP

SAFETY & SANITY IN THE FIELD.

LIFE IN THE FIELD!

SMELL THE LATRINES! TASTE HUMILITY! HEAR RODENTS! SEE THE ARMED GUERILLAS! FEEL YOUR SANITY SLIPPING!

WHILE SHANE IS DOING FIELDWORK IN AN INSTITUTION THAT IS FAMILIAR TO HER AND NOT "EXOTIC"...

& IN WHICH THE MOST DANGEROUS ENCOUNTER SHE MAY HAVE IS WITH A PAPERCUT,

OW!

NOT ALL BEGINNING FIELD WORKERS STUDY SO CLOSE TO HOME.

IT IS CRUCIAL FOR SAFETY, SUCCESS AND SANITY TO BE AWARE OF CULTURAL,

ENVIRONMENTAL,

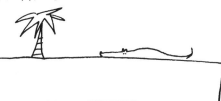

POLITICAL,

AND OTHER FACTORS

I HAVE TO WEAR WHAT?!?

AND, THERE ARE LOTS OF POLITICAL ISSUES FOR ETHNOGRAPHERS TO CONTEND WITH IN DOMESTIC AND WORKPLACE SETTINGS, TOO!

GOOD EATIN' NEVER HURT SO BAD!

AN ETHNOGRAPHER IN THE FIELD SURE WORKS UP AN APPETITE — BUT BEFORE CHOWING DOWN ON ANY CUISINE IN FAR-AWAY PLACES...

GET TO KNOW

HI!

THE MICROORGANISM,

THE PARASITIC WORM,

HI.

AND OTHERS. THE WORLD HEALTH ORG. IDENTIFIES 46 AGENTS OF INFECTION IN DRINKING WATER WORLDWIDE.

DEPENDING ON WHERE YOUR SITE IS, THE LOCAL FOOD & WATER MAY NOT BE WHAT YOU ARE USED TO.

WHILE THEY MAY NOT BOTHER THE LOCALS — YOU WILL EXPERIENCE THEIR FURY ON YOUR TENDER, WESTERN TUMMY.

COMMON WISDOM SUGGESTS DRINKING BOTTLED WATER...

GOT ANY BOTTLED WATER?

BUT IF YOU HAVE NO CHOICE, THAT'S JUST TOUGH.

MOST OF THE TIME YOU WON'T BE ABLE TO TELL BY LOOKING IF SOMETHING MAY MAKE YOU SICK.

BUT IN OTHER CASES IT WILL BE PAINFULLY OBVIOUS.

THE FOOD IS MOVING.

AND UNLESS YOU WANT TO HURT THE HOSTESS' FEELINGS,

I AM SO HONORED TO HAVE YOU HERE!

SUCK IT UP AND TAKE A NICE BIG BITE.

gulp!

BUT, NO MATTER WHAT YOU HAVE TO EAT OR DRINK...

SOME THINGS THAT MIGHT REALLY HELP INCLUDE:

TAKING YOUR OWN BOTTLED WATER ON SHORT TRIPS

FINDING A WESTERN DOCTOR IN THE AREA <u>BEFORE</u> YOU GET SICK.

STOCK UP ON ANTE-TUMMY-UPSET DRUGS

NO-PUKE Rx   KEEP IT DOWN Rx

OR EVEN FINDING SOME WATER-PURIFYING TABLETS—THOUGH THESE OFTEN DO NOT WORK & TASTE BAD...

YICK!

BUT, IF YOU DO NOT GET BETTER, OR IF YOU GET WORSE—

ugh.

SEE A DOCTOR, <u>ANY</u> DOCTOR, IMMEDIATELY!

moo?

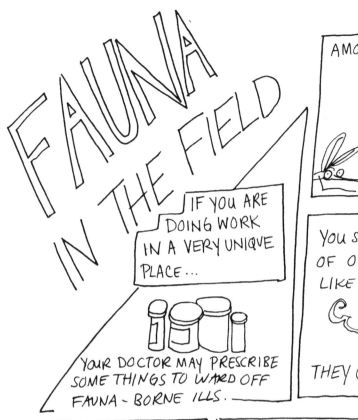

FAUNA IN THE FIELD

IF YOU ARE DOING WORK IN A VERY UNIQUE PLACE...

YOUR DOCTOR MAY PRESCRIBE SOME THINGS TO WARD OFF FAUNA-BORNE ILLS.

AMONG THEM, MALARIA AND OTHER MOSQUITO-BITE SPREAD BUGS.

YOU SHOULD ALSO BE WARY OF OTHER CREEPY CRAWLIES LIKE HOOKWORMS

OR ROUNDWORMS

THEY GET INTO A BODY VIA...

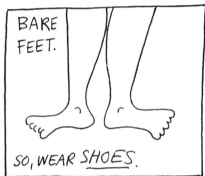

BARE FEET.

SO, WEAR <u>SHOES</u>.

EVEN WITH MEDICINE, SLEEPING UNDER A MOSQUITO NET IS ALWAYS A GOOD IDEA.

RABIES IS ENDEMIC TO MANY PARTS OF THE WORLD — SO DON'T PET THE ANIMALS.

NICE PUPPY

rrrrr

JUST FOLLOW THE ADVICE OF THE LOCAL FOLKS — AND YOU SHOULD BE OKAY.

AAAAA!

IT'S A GARDEN SNAKE.

A FEW SIMPLE RULES WILL KEEP YOU OUT OF HOT WATER.

BATH HOUSE

NO.

RESPECT THE CULTURAL GENDER NORMS OF THE COMMUNITY...

IT'S HOT IN HERE!

EVEN IF YOU DON'T AGREE WITH THEM.

SHANE, MAYBE YOU SHOULD DO THE INTERVIEWS WITH THE WOMEN.

& I'LL DO THE MEN?

BE AWARE OF THE IMPACT OF YOUR SEX ON THE DATA.

I THINK IT'S POSSIBLE HE FELT IT WOULD BE DISRESPECTFUL TO TALK ABOUT THAT WITH ME...

BE AWARE ALSO OF SPECIAL CONSIDERATIONS OR PRECAUTIONS RELATED TO YOUR SEX...

AND NO MATTER HOW TEMPTING...

NEVER COMPROMISE THE INTEGRITY OF YOUR STUDY BY LETTING SEX — WITH PARTICIPANTS OR ANYONE ELSE —

AH, SHANE — ZEE MOONLIGHT IN YOUR HAIR...

— GET IN THE WAY. IT'S NOT WORTH THE HEADACHE.

LOOK, THERE'S A POWER DIFFERENTIAL HERE — I'M THE RESEARCHER. PLUS, THE DATA...

SOB

ETHNOGRAPHIC DATA
COLLECTION METHODS!

THIS IS FOR JUST ONE OF MY QUESTIONS.

☆ REVISIT "PARADIGM CORRAL" FOR MORE ON SUBJECTIVITY

KEEPING A RESEARCHER JOURNAL CAN REALLY HELP WITH THIS.

IT CAN ALSO BE USEFUL LATER ON.

SO THAT'S WHAT I WAS THINKING.

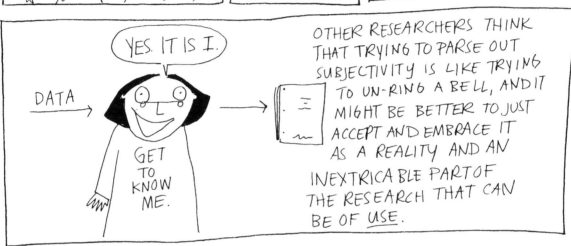

DATA

YES. IT IS I.

GET TO KNOW ME.

OTHER RESEARCHERS THINK THAT TRYING TO PARSE OUT SUBJECTIVITY IS LIKE TRYING TO UN-RING A BELL, AND IT MIGHT BE BETTER TO JUST ACCEPT AND EMBRACE IT AS A REALITY AND AN INEXTRICABLE PART OF THE RESEARCH THAT CAN BE OF USE.

DATA

NOT HERE. YOU DON'T SEE ME.

STILL OTHERS WANT TO THINK THERE ARE WAYS TO BE UTTERLY RID OF THIS FILTER — TO MINIMIZE IT OR BE RID OF IT ENTIRELY SO THAT THE STUDY IS TOTALLY "OBJECTIVE."★

HOW YOU FEEL WILL IMPACT HOW YOU COLLECT DATA (AND THINK!) (AND LATER ON, WRITE ABOUT YOUR DATA)

ETHNO AIRLINES

I'M SORRY, MA'AM, BUT YOU HAVE TOO MUCH SUBJECTIVE BAGGAGE TO BOARD THIS FLIGHT.

SELF IDEAS NOTIONS EXPERIENCES NORMATIVE ASSUMPTIONS

★ OF COURSE, YOU CAN'T EVER DO SOMETHING TOTALLY "OBJECTIVE" WHEN YOU ARE THE INSTRUMENT!

A PROFESSOR ONCE TOLD ME THAT IN POLICING YOUR SUBJECTIVITY, YOU SHOULD PAY CLOSE ATTENTION TO ANYTHING THAT PROVOKES

A STRONG REACTION — GOOD OR BAD — AND MAKE A NOTE OF IT.

I'M USING AT LEAST THREE KINDS OF DATA COLLECTION SO I CAN KIND OF COMPARE LATER ON.

method one — method two / method three

QUESTIONS SHOULD BE ANSWERED BY MORE THAN ONE DATA POINT — THAT WAY YOU CAN BE SURE OF YOUR FINDINGS

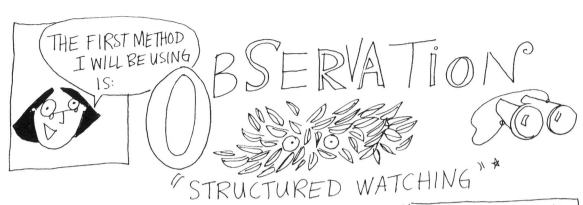

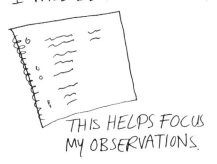

☆ USING UNOBTRUSIVE MEASURES

Field Notes

I TRY TO ORGANIZE MY FIELD NOTES A LITTLE BIT— I'VE TRIED A COUPLE OF DIFFERENT WAYS:

What is said	Actions
Q: "Is that your order of red tights?"	Standing by mailboxes, Dr. Q, Dr. O & Dr. Z.
O: "This?" (Laugh)	
Q: "Yeah—for your costume!"	
O: "No—this is my cape. The tights are on right now under my [pants]" (Laugh)	
Q: "You teach today?"	

	What I see	My reactions
	10:30	
	Dr. O had a package come from fedex -others	Collegial use of humor, an in-joke?
	asked if it was her new red tights with some laughter. She said it was her cape.	ha!
	More laughter.	
	10:40 Congregating at mailboxes, invitations to	mailboxes a gathering place?

↑ THIS WAY I CAN "SHELVE" MY SUBJECTIVITY— AND ALSO CHECK MY DEDUCTIONS OF MEANING IN INTERVIEWS LATER ON. (I USE PSEUDONYMS)

← THIS WAY I CAN SEPARATE VERBATIM WORDS AND ACTIONS, ETC.

NO MATTER HOW TIRED YOU ARE AT THE END OF EACH SESSION—YOU MUST TRANSCRIBE YOUR NOTES RIGHT AWAY!

WHILE YOU MIGHT SLEEP LIKE A BABY, WHEN THE SUN COMES UP....

WHAT YESTERDAY LOOKED LIKE THIS:

WILL, JUST 24 HOURS LATER, LOOK LIKE THIS:

AND YOU WILL LOOK LIKE THIS:

THE SAME GOES FOR ANY TAPE-RECORDINGS MADE DURING OBSERVATION. THE SOONER YOU TRANSCRIBE THEM...

THE MORE LIKELY IT IS YOU'LL IDENTIFY THINGS,

AND REMEMBER OTHER DETAILS.

ALSO, IF YOU DO TAPE-RECORD, BE SURE TO ALSO TAKE NOTES.

NOTES ALWAYS HELP... AND THINGS CAN SOMETIMES GO AWRY...

I'M GOING TO BE OBSERVING IN A COUPLE OF DIFFERENT CONTEXTS—

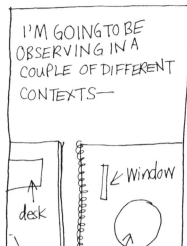

desk

Window

table

SOME OF THEM, LIKE THE FRONT OFFICE AT SCHOOL, ARE PUBLIC PLACES, SO—

I'M GOING TO TRY TO GET HOME BY 6.

I DON'T NEED TO ASK SPECIFIC PERMISSION—

I WAS HERE PRETTY LATE, TOO— I JUST CAN'T SEEM TO GET AWAY.

THERE'S NO EXPECTATION OF PRIVACY.

BUT OTHER CONTEXTS—LIKE IN A FACULTY MEETING—

SO, WHO WANTS TO CHAIR THIS COMMITTEE?

NOT IT.

—OR AT SOCIAL GATHERINGS IN A PRIVATE HOME, ETC. —

SO THERE I WAS IN HIS OFFICE!

I NEED TO ASK PERMISSION TO BE THERE AND TO TAKE NOTES;

I WOULD LIKE TO TAKE NOTES AND OBSERVE—BUT YOUR PRIVACY WILL BE PROTECTED WITH PSEUDONYMS...

AND *ESPECIALLY* IF I AUDIO OR VIDEOTAPE—

WHAT DO YOU MEAN YOU'RE GLAD YOU GOT THAT ON TAPE?

IN REVIEWING MY OBSERVATION, I LOOK FOR:

1. ANY QUESTIONS THAT MAY HAVE ARISEN, OR PATTERNS—THINGS I CAN ASK AN INFORMANT (i.e.,"interviewee") TO CLARIFY.

2. INDIVIDUALS WHO WOULD BE GOOD INFORMANTS. WHOSE PERSPECTIVE IS REPRESENTATIVE OR UNIQUE?

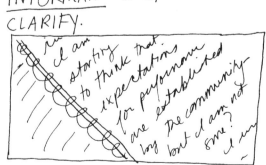

ARMED WITH MY CONCLUSIONS, I CONDUCT,

"PROBING CONVERSATIONS"

ETHNOGRAPHIC INTERVIEWING CAN BE <u>STRUCTURED</u>, <u>OPEN-ENDED</u> OR SOMEWHERE IN-BETWEEN!

open-ended INTERVIEWS ARE TYPICALLY:

Structured or Semi-Structured INTERVIEWS ARE TYPICALLY:

① EXPLORATORY

FLEXIBLE, BUT WITH FOCUSED, SPECIFIC QUESTIONS & APPROACH

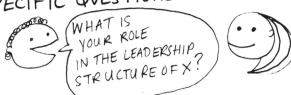

② OPEN TO A VARIETY OF RESPONSES

LOOKING FOR SPECIFIC DATA

③ ABOUT LEARNING ABOUT SOMETHING NEW & UNKNOWN

STRUCTURED TO HELP MAKE MORE SENSE OF SOMETHING ALREADY EXPLORED

④ UNSTRUCTURED OR ONLY SOMEWHAT <u>ORDERED IN FORMAT</u>

FEATURES A SET OF <u>ORDERED QUESTIONS</u>

LET'S COMPARE:

NORMAL CONVERSATION (VS.) ETHNOGRAPHIC INTERVIEW

WITH MOM...

ON A REALLY BAD DATE...

SEE? IT IS ABOUT GETTING INFORMATION FROM EITHER:

A. PEOPLE WHO ARE REPRESENTATIVE OF THE GROUP

OR

B. PEOPLE WITH UNIQUE PERSPECTIVES (KEY INFORMANTS)

PROVIDE BACKGROUND

WHAT'S THE HISTORY OF THE PROGRAM?

WELL...

PUT THINGS IN CATEGORIES

WHAT KINDS OF BEHAVIORS?

OH—THERE'S AVOIDANCE, TOPIC-CH...

OR ANY OTHER THINGS YOU WANT TO KNOW— YOU MAY EVEN COME UP WITH MORE QUESTIONS.

IN MORE STRUCTURED INTERVIEWS, INFORMANTS MAY BE ASKED TO RESPOND TO VIGNETTES OR OTHER "ELICITATION DEVICES."

REGARDLESS OF HOW YOU DO IT, BE SURE TO READ, REVIEW AND PRACTICE YOUR QUESTIONS WITH SOMEONE BEFORE THE REAL THING.

what was that, honey?

AND REMEMBER TO BRING:

IRB

YOUR INFORMED CONSENT FORMS

Field Notes

NOTEBOOK & PENS

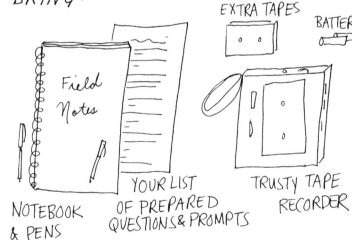

EXTRA TAPES

BATTERIES

YOUR LIST OF PREPARED QUESTIONS & PROMPTS

TRUSTY TAPE RECORDER

AND WHAT DO YOU DO THE **FIRST CHANCE** YOU GET?

I TRANSCRIBE FIELD NOTES AND TAPES WHILE IT'S FRESH IN MY MIND.

IT'S ALSO NOT A BAD IDEA TO GIVE INTERVIEW TRANSCRIPTS BACK TO INFORMANTS TO CHECK.

HMM... THAT DIDN'T COME ACROSS CLEARLY...

THIS IS CALLED "MEMBER CHECKING"

HOW MANY INTERVIEWS DO YOU PLAN TO DO?

BECAUSE THE GROUP IS PRETTY SMALL...

... IN ORDER TO GET A TRULY REPRESENTATIVE COLLECTION OF INTERVIEWS, I NEED TO GET AS MANY AS I CAN. IF IT WAS A BIGGER GROUP, I'D HAVE TO GET A SAMPLE.*

MY THIRD DATA SOURCE WILL COMPLEMENT THESE INTERVIEWS AND MY OBSERVATIONS.

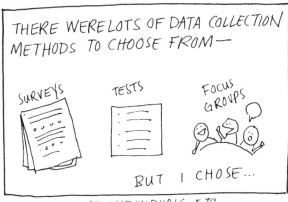

THERE WERE LOTS OF DATA COLLECTION METHODS TO CHOOSE FROM—

SURVEYS   TESTS   FOCUS GROUPS

BUT I CHOSE...

☆ REFER BACK TO OUR DISCUSSION OF SAMPLING GROUPS, INDIVIDUALS, ETC.

ARTIFACT COLLECTION

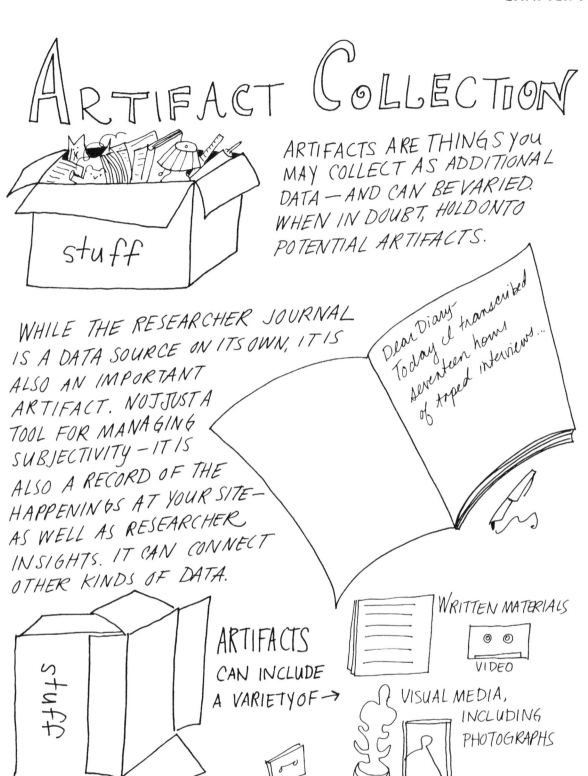

ARTIFACTS ARE THINGS YOU MAY COLLECT AS ADDITIONAL DATA — AND CAN BE VARIED. WHEN IN DOUBT, HOLD ONTO POTENTIAL ARTIFACTS.

WHILE THE RESEARCHER JOURNAL IS A DATA SOURCE ON ITS OWN, IT IS ALSO AN IMPORTANT ARTIFACT. NOT JUST A TOOL FOR MANAGING SUBJECTIVITY — IT IS ALSO A RECORD OF THE HAPPENINGS AT YOUR SITE — AS WELL AS RESEARCHER INSIGHTS. IT CAN CONNECT OTHER KINDS OF DATA.

Dear Diary—
Today I transcribed seventeen hours of taped interviews...

stuff

ARTIFACTS CAN INCLUDE A VARIETY OF →

WRITTEN MATERIALS

VIDEO

VISUAL MEDIA, INCLUDING PHOTOGRAPHS

AUDIO

OBJECTS

... AND ALMOST ANYTHING ELSE

FOR MY STUDY, I WILL BE COLLECTING A LOT OF WRITTEN MATERIALS.

COURSE SYLLABI ...

MEETING NOTES & MINUTES

PERSONAL COMMUNICATION

even e-mails!

AND I WILL TAKE & COLLECT PHOTOGRAPHS, AS WELL AS ENLIST PARTICIPANTS TO PHOTOGRAPH THINGS IMPORTANT TO THEM.

OF COURSE - WHAT AN "ARTIFACT" MIGHT LOOK LIKE MAY VARY SITE BY SITE...

BUT ARTIFACTS CAN BE USED TO DEVELOP THEMES, REGARDLESS. SOMETIMES USING ARTIFACTS AS PART OF DATA IS CALLED "CONTENT ANALYSIS."

OKAY - HOW DO YOU KNOW WHEN YOU ARE DONE COLLECTING DATA?

REMEMBER WHEN I TALKED ABOUT HAVING MORE THAN ONE METHOD?

WELL, I WILL STOP DATA COLLECTION WHEN I'M GETTING ANSWERS TO MY QUESTIONS THAT ARE CONSISTENT IN SEVERAL DIFFERENT PLACES.* OF COURSE, I CAN ALWAYS COLLECT MORE LATER, TOO...

WHAT HAPPENS NEXT?

* WHEN YOU KEEP SEEING THE SAME THING OVER AND OVER AGAIN, YOU'VE REACHED WHAT IS CALLED "SATURATION."

DEALING WITH & ANALYZING
THE DATA

SHANE HAS BEEN COLLECTING DATA FOR A WHILE AND IS NOW STARTING TO CONTEMPLATE THE NEXT STEP.

WELL, SANJ—I HAD SUCH A HANDLE ON DATA COLLECTION, I DID A REALLY GOOD JOB.

NOPE—STILL CAN'T FIND THE FLOOR.

YEAH — DATA COLLECTION WAS SO GREAT—I REALLY GOT IT, BUT I DON'T QUITE SEE THE NEXT STEP...

ANALYSIS.

SHANE HAD YET AGAIN GOTTEN HERSELF IN A PICKLE.

I DON'T KNOW WHAT TO DO WITH ALL THIS STUFF!

BEFORE YOU EVEN THINK ABOUT ANALYSIS, CONSIDER TAKING STOCK OF WHAT'S HERE — NO PUN INTENDED...

...AND TAKING SOME TIME TO DO SOME ORGANIZING AND SAFEGUARDING OF DATA.

TRANSCRIPTS COPIES COPIES OF COPIES

IF YOU HAVE ANY TROUBLE MOTIVATING YOURSELF TO DO THIS,

I SWORE THEY WERE IN THIS BOX!

A.   A.

JUST IMAGINE LOSING YOUR DATA.

I LOST MY FIELDNOTES! NOOOOOOOOoooo..!!!

LET THE NIGHTMARE BEGIN!

YOU CAN PREVENT THIS HORROR OF HORRORS BY USING THE SIMPLE SORTING SYSTEM INVOLVING SIMPLE STEPS:

USING —

YOUR SALVATION, THE MIGHTY COPY MACHINE

COPY REX

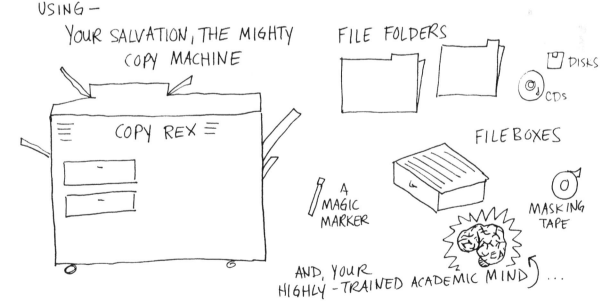

FILE FOLDERS

DISKS

CDS

FILE BOXES

A MAGIC MARKER

MASKING TAPE

AND, YOUR HIGHLY-TRAINED ACADEMIC MIND ...

SO BEGINS ANALYSIS

DATA ANALYSIS IS MOSTLY A PROCESS OF SIFTING AND THINKING AND WAITING...

... FOR PATTERNS TO EMERGE.

I KEEP SEEING THE SAME THING ACROSS METHODS...

YOUR JOURNAL CAN HELP YOU TRACK YOUR HUNCHES THROUGH THE PROCESS.

BIG PILES OF DATA

GET MASSAGED INTO SMALLER PILES OF DATA★ THAT END UP ANSWERING YOUR QUESTIONS.

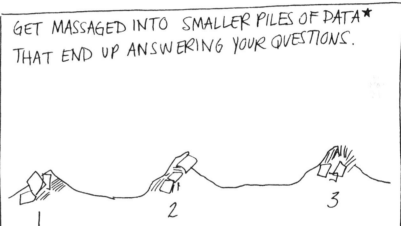

AS THESE SMALL PILES FORM, YOU'LL KEEP LOOKING FOR PATTERNS AND THEMES.

KINDS OF TALK

YOU MAY EVEN RETURN TO THE FIELD TO "DOUBLE CHECK".

I'M SEEING THE SAME THING — JUST AS THE DATA SUGGEST.

★ THIS GOOD IDEA FROM LECOMPTE & SCHENSUL (1999)

ANALYSIS CAN INVOLVE TECHNOLOGY... HIGH-TECH, LOW-TECH & NO-TECH.

NOW THAT YOU'VE "TIDIED UP" YOUR DATA, LET'S THINK A LITTLE MORE DEEPLY ABOUT DOING THE ACTUAL ANALYSIS:

DATA ANALYSIS 101! ROLL UP YER SLEEVES!

YOU CAN THINK ABOUT DATA ANALYSIS AS A PROCESS WHERE YOU FOCUS WHAT THE DATA ARE "SAYING" TO YOU.

YOU BEGIN WITH ORDERING THE DATA INTO THE PILES WE TALKED ABOUT.

THE NEXT THING YOU WILL DO IS IDENTIFY PATTERNS IN THE PILES OF DATA...

... AND THEN LOOKING FOR RELATIONSHIPS BETWEEN AND ACROSS THESE PATTERNS.

IN ETHNOGRAPHY, THE PROCESS OF DATA ANALYSIS CAN BE OPEN-ENDED AND QUITE INDIVIDUALIZED. THIS IS ONE REASON WHY TRIANGULATION AND MEMBER-CHECKING ARE IMPORTANT TO DOUBLECHECK FINDINGS.

BUT JUST BECAUSE IT IS OPEN-ENDED, THIS DOESN'T MEAN THE PROCESS IS IN ANY WAY UNDISCIPLINED!

ANALYSIS OF ETHNOGRAPHIC DATA HAPPENS IN A DISCIPLINED WAY IN 3 PARTS (TYPICALLY).

1. ANALYSIS DONE WHILE DATA ARE STILL BEING COLLECTED IN THE FIELD

2. ANALYSIS DONE RIGHT AT COMPLETION OF STUDY, WHILE YOU ARE EITHER IN THE FIELD OR JUST AFTER YOU STOP DATA COLLECTION.

3 ANALYSIS DONE AFTER YOU'VE BEEN OUT OF THE FIELD FOR A LITTLE WHILE.

LECOMPTE & SCHENSUL (1999)
TALK ABOUT THESE THREE
"PHASES" OF DATA COLLECTION
IN THESE TERMS

1. IN-THE-FIELD ANALYSIS:
   ★ GOING OVER DATA WHILE
     STILL IN "COLLECTION MODE"
   ★ MAKING MENTAL NOTES
   ★ ATTENDING TO SUBJECTIVITY
   ★ PRODUCING DESCRIPTIONS
   ★ FIELDNOTES

3. "COOKING" THE "RAW" DATA
   TO MAKE IT INTO RESEARCH
   RESULTS.*

2. "TIDYING UP" DATA UPON
   RETURN FROM THE FIELD:
   (WE'VE ALREADY TALKED A
   BIT ABOUT THIS — IT
   INCLUDES SORTING, SAFE-
   GUARDING & COPYING, ETC.)

THERE ARE TWO WAYS TO THINK ABOUT DOING #3 DATA ANALYSIS:

"TOP-DOWN"   &   "BOTTOM-UP"

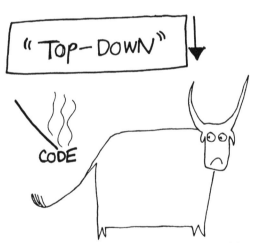

CODE

THINK OF TOP-DOWN ANALYSIS
AS THE APPLICATION OF
"CODES" YOU'VE COME
UP WITH TO THE DATA
AS A WAY TO HELP YOU
SORT AND MAKE SENSE OF
RELATIONSHIPS ACROSS
AND BETWEEN THE DATA.

THINK OF BOTTOM-UP ANALYSIS
AS MORE INDUCTIVE THAN
TOP-DOWN WORK, AND THAT
IT INVOLVES WORKING OUT
IN THE RESEARCHER'S HEAD
WHAT'S GOING ON IN THE DATA.
AFTER EXTENSIVE READING
AND RE-READING, OR RE-
EXAMINING THE DATA,
CODES ARE GENERATED FROM
THE DATA

* NOT TO BE CONFUSED WITH "COOKING THE DATA" AS RESULT FABRICATION!

LOOKING MORE CLOSELY AT
TOP-DOWN ANALYSIS:

YOUR "CODES" — THE TERMS
AND THEMES YOU USE TO SORT
YOUR DATA — CAN COME
FROM YOUR CONCEPTUAL
FRAMEWORK AND RESEARCH
QUESTIONS. (REMEMBER, WE
SAID YOU NEEDED A FRAMEWORK!!!)

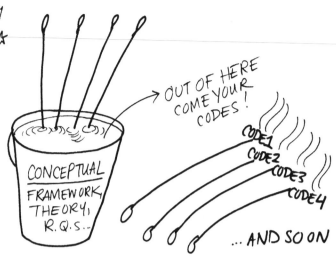

OUT OF HERE
COME YOUR
CODES!

CODE1
CODE2
CODE3
CODE4

... AND SO ON

CONCEPTUAL
FRAMEWORK,
THEORY,
R.Q.s...

SO, OUT OF YOUR "HERD"
OF DATA..

moo   moooo   Moooooooo

... COME CODED DATA!

CODE1   CODE2   CODE3

CODES AND THEIR MEANINGS ARE KEPT IN A "CODEBOOK" — WHICH IS
GOOD TO KEEP HANDY THROUGHOUT ANALYSIS.

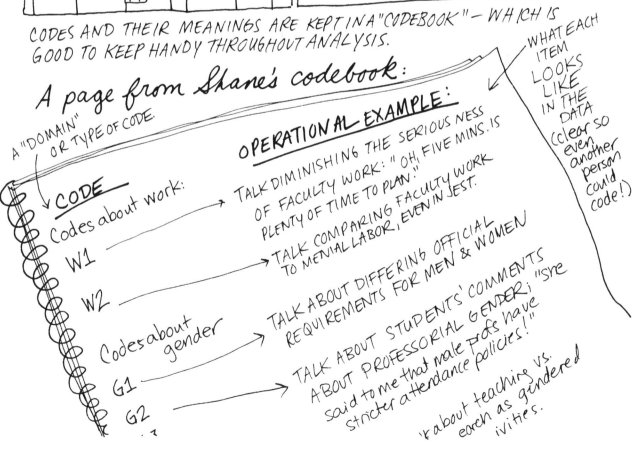

A page from Shane's codebook:

WHAT EACH
ITEM
LOOKS
LIKE
IN THE
DATA
(clear so
even
another
person
could
code!)

A "DOMAIN" OR TYPE OF CODE.

CODE
Codes about work:

W1 ——→ TALK DIMINISHING THE SERIOUSNESS
OF FACULTY WORK: "OH, FIVE MINS. IS
PLENTY OF TIME TO PLAN."

OPERATIONAL EXAMPLE:

W2 ——→ TALK COMPARING FACULTY WORK
TO MENIAL LABOR, EVEN IN JEST.

Codes about
gender ——→ TALK ABOUT DIFFERING OFFICIAL
REQUIREMENTS FOR MEN & WOMEN

G1 ——→ TALK ABOUT STUDENTS' COMMENTS
ABOUT PROFESSORIAL GENDER; "SHE
said to me that male profs have
stricter attendance policies!"

G2 ——→ 'k about teaching vs.
earch as gendered
ivities.

NOW LET'S TAKE A LOOK AT "BOTTOM-UP" ANALYSIS:

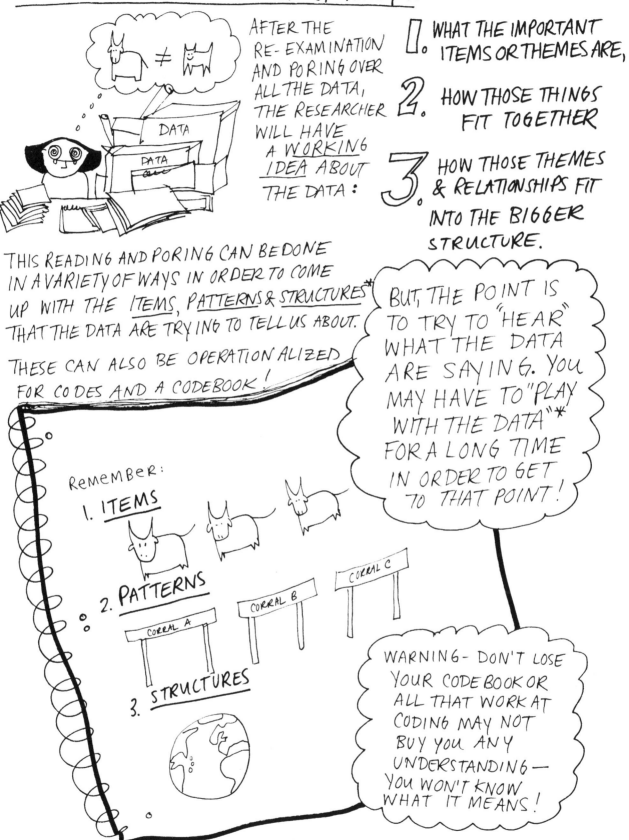

AFTER THE RE-EXAMINATION AND PORING OVER ALL THE DATA, THE RESEARCHER WILL HAVE A <u>WORKING IDEA</u> ABOUT THE DATA:

1. WHAT THE IMPORTANT ITEMS OR THEMES ARE,

2. HOW THOSE THINGS FIT TOGETHER

3. HOW THOSE THEMES & RELATIONSHIPS FIT INTO THE BIGGER STRUCTURE.

THIS READING AND PORING CAN BE DONE IN A VARIETY OF WAYS IN ORDER TO COME UP WITH THE <u>ITEMS</u>, <u>PATTERNS</u> & <u>STRUCTURES</u>* THAT THE DATA ARE TRYING TO TELL US ABOUT.

THESE CAN ALSO BE OPERATIONALIZED FOR CODES AND A CODEBOOK!

BUT, THE POINT IS TO TRY TO "HEAR" WHAT THE DATA ARE SAYING. YOU MAY HAVE TO "PLAY WITH THE DATA"* FOR A LONG TIME IN ORDER TO GET TO THAT POINT!

Remember:

1. ITEMS

2. PATTERNS

CORRAL A   CORRAL B   CORRAL C

3. STRUCTURES

WARNING- DON'T LOSE YOUR CODEBOOK OR ALL THAT WORK AT CODING MAY NOT BUY YOU ANY UNDERSTANDING— YOU WON'T KNOW WHAT IT MEANS!

DATA   DATA

* LECOMPTE & SCHENSUL (1999) CAME UP WITH THIS TURN OF PHRASE!

TYPICALLY, PEOPLE CODE WITH PENS, PENCILS & HIGHLIGHTERS,*
GOING THROUGH NOTES, TRANSCRIPTS OR OTHER DATA AND
NOTING WHAT IS WHAT USING CODES FROM THE CODEBOOK.
(IT IS TIME CONSUMING, BUT IF YOU FIND THAT YOUR CODES
AREN'T "WORKING", GO BACK AND CHECK BOTH YOUR OWN
UNDERSTANDING OF THE CONSTRUCTS AND THE WAY YOU
HAVE OPERATIONALIZED YOUR CODES.)

a page of Shane's data:

"Naked" (uncoded)

Interviewer: Okay, can you tell me more about that? Can you list the parts of that kind of work?
Participant: Well, committee work is a lot like mothering, actually—you have the baby on your hip and the dinner on the stove and the TV on and soccer practice at 4 and the phone is ringing—in other words it's multitasking at its most intense. There's actual meeting time, prepping for the meeting, talking with stakeholders outside of the meeting before and after, keeping abreast of current campus concerns and also finding time to think critically about what's going on. It's a lot.
Interviewer: How long have you been involved in this kind of work outside of regular academic responsibilities?
Participant: The past six years.
Interviewer: How many hours a week are you involved in working outside of department like this?
Participant: I'd say 15-2 hours. But this is a pretty intense experience. Everyone does out of department stuff but not everyone has that kind of time commitment.
Interviewer: What do you think is the impact of this level of intense work on the culture of the department?
Participant: I think it serves to make us much less cohesive, much more likely to go into our offices and shut our doors because we're all so busy, every 15 minutes is precious, you know?
Interviewer: Uh-huh. Can you describe what it feels like to work in that kind of office culture?
Participant: People respect your time, that's great, but I wonder if we could be more of a real community—have more meaningful dialogue if we weren't so

Coded!

Interviewer: Okay, can you tell me more about that? Can you list the parts of that kind of work?
Participant: Well, committee work is a lot like mothering, actually—[you have the baby on your hip and the dinner on the stove and the TV on and soccer practice at 4 and the phone is ringing—in other words it's multitasking at its most intense.] There's actual meeting time, prepping for the meeting, talking with stakeholders outside of the meeting before and after, keeping abreast of current campus concerns and also finding time to think critically about what's going on. It's a lot. — M6
Interviewer: How long have you been involved in this kind of work outside of regular academic responsibilities?
Participant: The past six years.
Interviewer: How many hours a week are you involved in working outside of department like this?
Participant: I'd say 15-2 hours. But this is a pretty intense experience. Everyone does out of department stuff but not everyone has that kind of time commitment.
Interviewer: What do you think is the impact of this level of intense work on the culture of the department?
Participant: I think it serves to make us much less cohesive, much more likely to go into our offices and shut our doors because we're all so busy, every 15 minutes is precious, you know?
Interviewer: Uh-huh. Can you describe what it feels like to work in that kind of office culture?
Participant: People respect your time, that's great, but I wonder if we could be more of a real community—have more meaningful dialogue if we weren't so

Coded annotations (handwritten): M1, M1a, M12 G12 · T1a · T3b · T1b · M6 · T2u · F1a · Mb1 · F2 · S4 · dub · double-check—meant 20? · S3 · T1a · Q1a, R3 M1a · S4 · W4, W3 · P3, P6 R6, R7

See WHY SHANE WILL NEED HER CODE-BOOK?

* OR SCISSORS & TAPE, OR COMPUTER PROGRAMS!

1. THE THEORETICAL / CONCEPTUAL FRAMEWORK
&
2. YOUR RESEARCH QUESTIONS

AS YOU BEGIN WRITING ABOUT WHAT YOU FOUND.

NOW THAT SOME PATTERNS HAVE STARTED TO EMERGE, YOU CAN THINK ABOUT WRITING UP YOUR REPORT OF FINDINGS

OF COURSE - ONE'S IDEA OF THE PURPOSE OF THE ETHNOGRAPHY INFLUENCES THE WRITEUP!

THIS IS THE PART ABOUT THICK DESCRIPTION?

RIGHT.

THE ROLE OF THE ETHNOGRAPHER AS AN INTERPRETER OF CULTURE IS TO REPORT NOT ISOLATED PHYSICAL HAPPENINGS BUT RATHER _Meaning_

IN ORDER TO WRITE ABOUT - OR EVEN IMAGINE - THE POSSIBLE MEANINGS OF THINGS, YOU NEED TO THINK AS ETHNOGRAPHY AS "THICK DESCRIPTION."

THERE ARE THINGS GOING ON BEYOND THE APPARENT.

OBSERVED ACT (TIP OF THE ICEBERG)

CONTEXT & MEANING

WHEN YOU WRITE - AND DO - ETHNOGRAPHY, YOU'RE NOT "BOILING DOWN" - YOU'RE TELLING THE WHOLE STORY!

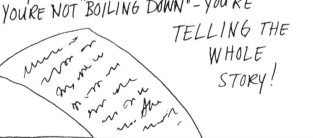

CONTEXT, LIFE AND MEANING!

THAT'S A LOT.

IN INVESTIGATING MEANING—IT IS IMPORTANT FOR ALL RESEARCHERS TO TAKE PRECAUTIONS THAT INSURE THE STRENGTH OF ANY STUDY, AND SUBSEQUENTLY OF THE FINDINGS. WE CALL THESE: {RELIABILITY} AND {VALIDITY}

THIS ASKS US, "CAN THIS STUDY BE REPEATED BY OTHER PEOPLE IN OTHER PLACES AND GET SIMILAR RESULTS?"

THIS ASKS US, "DID WE REALLY FIND WHAT WE THINK WE DID?" AND "HOW MEANINGFUL ARE OUR RESULTS?"

BUT, YOU CAN'T REALLY REPEAT AN ETHNOGRAPHY! SO, ETHNOGRAPHERS LOOK AT THIS AS:

BUT, WHEN YOU ARE THE INSTRUMENT IN A NATURALISTIC SETTING, WHAT IS VALIDITY? ETHNOGRAPHERS DEFINE IT LIKE THIS:

INTERNAL RELIABILITY:
DO THE IDEAS WE CAME UP WITH "MATCH" THE DATA?

&

EXTERNAL RELIABILITY:
HOW SIMILAR ARE FINDINGS IN OTHER STUDIES THAT USED THE SAME METHOD?

INTERNAL VALIDITY:
DO THE DATA COLLECTION METHODS REALLY DO A GOOD JOB REPRESENTING THE FIELD?

CONSTRUCT VALIDITY:
DO MEASURES (INTERVIEWS, ETC.) REALLY "GET AT" WHAT WE THINK THEY DO?

&

EXTERNAL VALIDITY:
CAN THESE DATA COLLECTION TECHNIQUES & CONSTRUCTS DESCRIBE GROUPS IN OTHER STUDIES?

WRITING UP YOUR RESULTS!

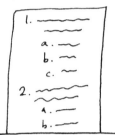

MUCH LATER

THERE'S NO REASON MY WRITEUP SHOULD BE ANY DIFFERENT...

THE PROFESSORS OF THAT DEPARTMENT HAD A LONG HISTORY OF LOW LIVING...

WELL, A LITTLE DIFFERENT...

I COULD EVEN CALL IT "THE GOOD, THE BAD AND THE ADJUNCT"...

PROBABLY NOT.

SO, I COULD START WITH AN OPENING VIGNETTE FROM MY FIELD NOTES...

MODELING COLLEGIALITY FOR STUDENTS, PROFESSOR X CHATS FROM THE CLASSROOM DOOR...

AND THEN MOVE ON TO TALK ABOUT EACH OF MY RESEARCH QUESTIONS,

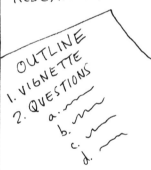

OUTLINE
1. VIGNETTE
2. QUESTIONS
   a.
   b.
   c.
   d.

TALKING ABOUT THE ANSWERS I FOUND,

3. FINDINGS
   a.
   b.
   c.
   d.

AND HOW I FOUND THEM.

4. METHODS
   a.
   b.
   c.

WOW—THIS THING IS REALLY WRITING ITSELF!

RIO BRAVO

... AND THAT'S A GOOD SIGN! BUT NOT EVERYBODY'S WRITING-UP PROCESS IS AS SMOOTH.

THERE ARE A FEW TRICKS OF THE TRADE THAT EVERYONE SHOULD KNOW TO HELP THEM THROUGH THE ROUGH PATCHES.

LIKE TRAIL DUST IN YOUR KNICKERS, A POOR ETHNOGRAPHIC WRITEUP MAKES FOR A LONG, HARD JOURNEY.

(DATA & ANALYSIS ALONE WON'T CUT IT.)

SHANE STARTED HER ETHNOGRAPHY WITH A NICE VIGNETTE ABOUT A PARTICULAR INCIDENT FROM THE FIELD. SHE KNOWS SHE IS "TELLING A GOOD STORY" ★ ABOUT THE DATA.

OTHER PEOPLE NEED TO GET MORE OF A "GRIP" ON THE DATA BEFORE THEY BEGIN TO WRITE, AND ONE WAY TO DO THAT IS TO MAP OUT, LITERALLY, WHAT YOUR "STORY" IS.

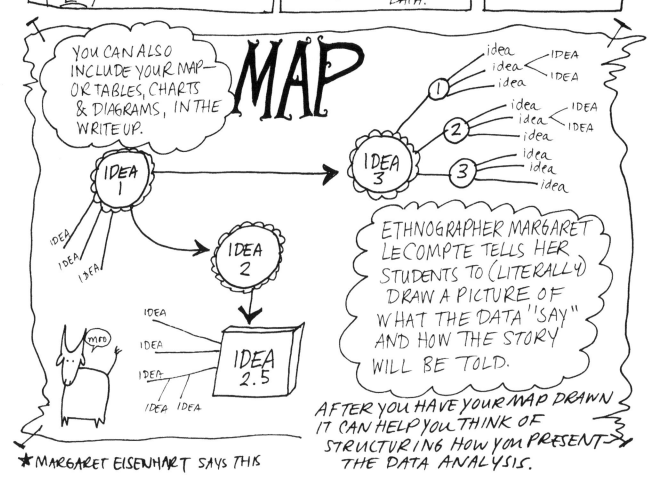

YOU CAN ALSO INCLUDE YOUR MAP—OR TABLES, CHARTS & DIAGRAMS, IN THE WRITEUP.

MAP

ETHNOGRAPHER MARGARET LECOMPTE TELLS HER STUDENTS TO (LITERALLY) DRAW A PICTURE OF WHAT THE DATA "SAY" AND HOW THE STORY WILL BE TOLD.

AFTER YOU HAVE YOUR MAP DRAWN IT CAN HELP YOU THINK OF STRUCTURING HOW YOU PRESENT THE DATA ANALYSIS.

★ MARGARET EISENHART SAYS THIS

Final Thoughts

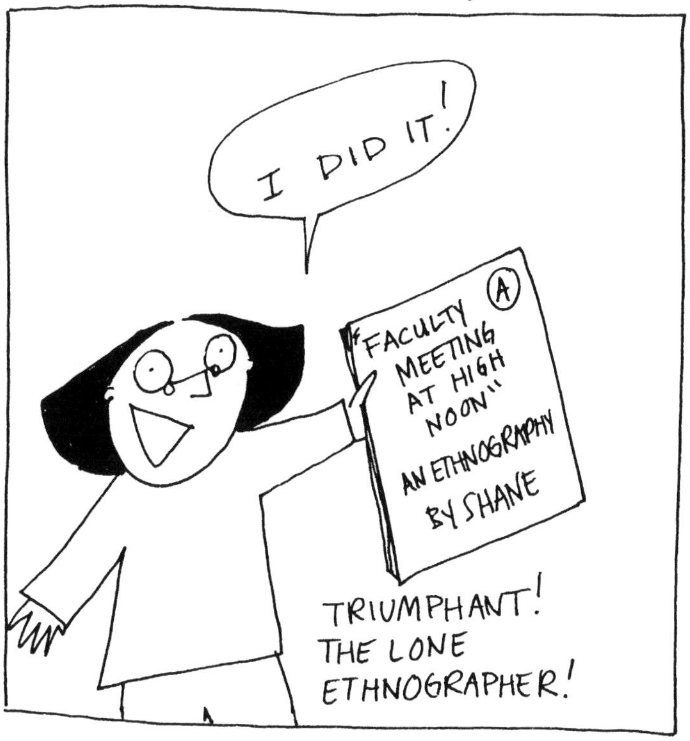

ETHNOGRAPHY

A → Z

FOR THOSE WHO DON'T WANT
TO GO IT ALONE!

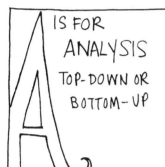

A IS FOR
ANALYSIS
TOP-DOWN OR
BOTTOM-UP

B IS FOR
FRANZ
BOAS
"cultural relativism"

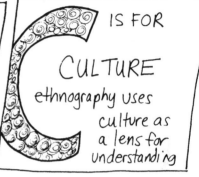

C IS FOR
CULTURE
ethnography uses
culture as
a lens for
understanding

D IS FOR DATA
ETHNOGRAPHY
USES A
WIDE
VARIETY
OF
DATA
(interviews, etc.)

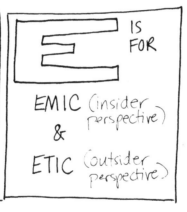

E IS
FOR
EMIC (insider perspective)
&
ETIC (outsider perspective)

F IS FOR
FIELDNOTES

You will collect
lots and lots of
fieldnotes!

G IS
FOR
CLIFFORD
GEERTZ
"thick description"

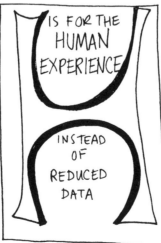

H IS FOR THE
HUMAN
EXPERIENCE

INSTEAD
OF
REDUCED
DATA

I IS FOR THE
I. R. B.

protecting
human
research
subjects!

J IS FOR JOURNAL

A GOOD RESEARCH TOOL!

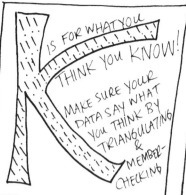

K IS FOR WHAT YOU THINK YOU KNOW! MAKE SURE YOUR DATA SAY WHAT YOU THINK BY TRIANGULATING & MEMBER-CHECKING

L IS FOR LITERATURE REVIEW

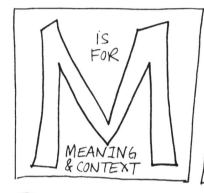

M IS FOR MEANING & CONTEXT

N IS FOR NATURALISTIC SETTING

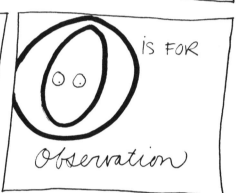

O IS FOR Observation

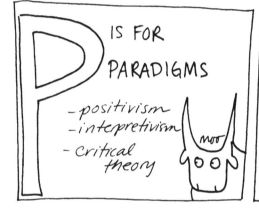

P IS FOR PARADIGMS

- positivism
- interpretivism
- critical theory

Q IS FOR A GOOD RESEARCH Question

R IS FOR RELIABILITY

REPLICATION OF RESEARCH RESULTS OVER TIME

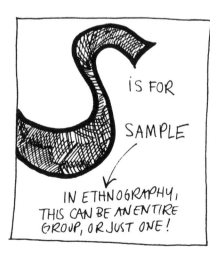

S IS FOR SAMPLE

IN ETHNOGRAPHY, THIS CAN BE AN ENTIRE GROUP, OR JUST ONE!

T IS FOR THEORY

- THEORETICAL FRAMEWORK
- ETHNOGRAPHY MAKES & IS GUIDED BY THEORY

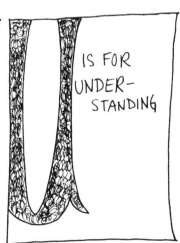

U IS FOR UNDER-STANDING

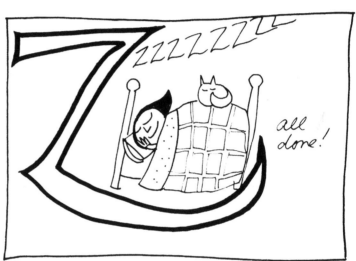

FURTHER READING

Adler, P. & Adler, P. A. (1987). *Membership roles in field research*. Newbury Park, CA: Sage Publications.

Agar, M. H. (1980). *The professional stranger: An informal introduction to ethnography*. New York: Academic Press.

Ammar, H. (1954). *Growing up in an Egyptian village: Silwa, province of Aswan*. London: Routledge.

Anderson, G. L. (1989). Critical ethnography in education: Origins, current status and new directions. *Review of Educational Research, 59* (3), 249–70.

Au, K. H. (1980). Participation structures in a reading lesson with Hawaiian children: Analysis of a culturally appropriate instruction event. *Anthropology and Education Quarterly, 11*, 91–115.

Becker, H. S., Geer, B., Hughes, E. C. & Strauss, A. L., (1961). *Boys in white: Student culture in medical school*. Chicago, IL: University of Chicago Press.

Benedict, R. (1934). *Patterns of culture*. Boston, MA: Houghton Mifflin.

Benedict, R. (1946). *The chrysanthemum and the sword: Patterns of Japanese culture*. Boston, MA: Houghton Mifflin.

Bernstein, B. B. (1971). *Class, codes and control*. London: Routledge.

Boas, F. (1928). *Anthropology and modern life*. New York: Norton.

Boas, F. (1940). *Race, language and culture*. Chicago, IL: University of Chicago Press.

Boas, F. & Codere, H. (1966). *Kwakiutl ethnography*. Chicago, IL: University of Chicago Press.

Bogdan, R. C. & Biklen, S. K. (1992). *Qualitative research for education: An introduction to theory and methods*. Boston, MA: Allyn & Bacon.

Borman, K. M. (1991). *The first "real" job: A study of young workers*. Albany, NY: SUNY Press.

Campbell, A. (1984). *The girls in the gang: A report from New York City*. New York: Basil Blackwell.

Campbell, S. A. (2005). *Ariadne's thread: Pre-service teachers, stories and identity in the teacher education context*. Unpublished doctoral dissertation: University of Colorado–Boulder.

Chagnon, M. A. (1974). *Studying the Yanomamo*. New York: Holt, Rinehart & Winston.

Chang, H. (1991). *American high school life and ethos: An ethnography*. New York: Falmer Press.

Delamont, S. (2002) *Fieldwork in educational settings: Methods, pitfalls and perspectives* (2nd ed.). London: Routledge.

Deyhle, D. M. (1991). Empowerment and cultural conflict: Navajo parents and the schooling of their children. *Qualitative Studies in Education*, 4, 277–97.

Eisenhart, M. A. & Graue, M. E. (1990). Socially constructed readiness for school. *Qualitative Studies in Education*, 3(3), 253–69.

Eisenhart, M. A. & Holland, D. C. (1990). Gender constructs and career choice: The influence of peer culture on women's commitments in college. In A. Whitehead & B. Reid (Eds.) *The cultural construction of gender*. Champaign, IL: University of Illinois Press.

Eisenhart, M. A. & Howe K. R. (1992). Validity in educational research. In M. D. LeCompte, W. L. Millroy & J. Preissle (Eds.), *The handbook of qualitative research in education* (pp. 643–80). San Diego, CA: Academic Press.

Evans-Pritchard, E. E. (1951). *Kinship and marriage among the Nuer*. Oxford: Oxford University Press.

Fine, M. & Zane, N. (1989). Bein' wrapped too tight: Why low-income women drop out of high school. In L. Weis, E. Farrar & H. Petrie (Eds.) *Dropouts from school: Issues, dilemmas and solutions*. Albany, NY: SUNY Press.

Fordham, S. (1993). "Those loud Black girls": (Black) women, silence, and gender "passing" in the academy. *Anthropology and Education Quarterly*, 24, 3-32.

Fordham, S. (1996). *Blacked out: Dilemmas of race, identity and success at capital high*. Chicago, IL: University of Chicago Press.

Geertz, C. (1973). *The interpretation of cultures: Selected essays*. New York: Basic Books.

Geertz, C. (1983). *Local knowledge: Further essays in interpretive anthropology*. New York: Basic Books.

Geertz, C. (1988). *Works and lives: The anthropologist as author*. Stanford, CA: Stanford University Press.

Gibson, M. A. (1988). *Accommodation without assimilation: Sikh immigrants in an American high school*. Ithaca, NY: Cornell University Press.

Glaser, B. G. & Strauss, A. L. (1965). *Awareness of dying*. Chicago: Aldine Publishing Co.

Goetz, J. P. & LeCompte, M. D. (November, 1978). *Data crunching: Techniques for analyzing field note data*. Paper presented at the Conference on Educational Evaluation, American Anthropological Association, Los Angeles, CA.

Goetz, J. P. & LeCompte, M. D. (1981). Ethnographic research and the problem of data reduction: What do I do with the five drawers of field notes? *Anthropology and Education Quarterly*, Vol. 12, No. 1, Spring, pp. 51–70.

Guba, E. G. (1981). Critique for assessing the trustworthiness of naturalistic inquiries. *ERIC/ECTJ Annual Review*, 29 (2), 75-91.

Holland, D. C. & Eisenhart, M. A. (1990). *Educated in romance: Women, achievement and college culture*. Chicago, IL: University of Chicago Press.

Lather, P. & Smithies, C. (1997). *Troubling the angels: Women living with HIV/AIDS*. Boulder, CO: Westview Press.

LeCompte, M. D., Millroy, W. L. & Preissle, J. (Eds.) (1992). *The handbook of qualitative research in education*. (pp. 447–98). San Diego, CA: Harcourt Brace.

LeCompte, M. D. & Goetz, J. (1982) Problems of reliability and validity in ethnographic research. *Review of Educational Research*, 52, pp. 31–60.

LeCompte, M. D. & Preissle, J. (1993). *Ethnography and qualitative design in educational research*. 2nd ed. New York, NY: Academic Press.

LeCompte, M. D., Preissle, J. & Tesch, R. (1993). *Ethnography and qualitative design in educational research*. San Diego, CA: Academic Press.

LeCompte, M. D. & Schensul, J. J. (1999). *Designing and conducting ethnographic research*. Vol. 1 in *The ethnographer's toolkit*. Walnut Creek, CA: AltaMira Press.

LeCompte, M. D. & Schensul, J. J. (1999). *Analyzing and interpreting ethnographic data*. Vol. 5 in *The ethnographer's toolkit*. Walnut Creek, CA: AltaMira Press.

LeCompte, M. D., Schensul, J. J., Weeks, M. R & Singer, M. (1999). *Researcher roles and research partnerships.* Vol. 6 in *The ethnographer's toolkit.* Walnut Creek, CA: AltaMira Press.

LeCompte, M. D. (2002). The transformation of ethnographic practice: Past and current challenges. *Qualitative Research,* (2) 3.

Levine, S. W. (2003). *Mystics, mavericks and merrymakers: An intimate journey among Hasidic girls.* New York: New York University Press.

Levinson, B. A. & Holland, D. C. (1996). *The cultural production of the educated person: Critical ethnographies of schooling and local practice.* Albany, NY: SUNY Press.

Lightfoot, S. L. (1983). *The good high school: Portraits of character and culture.* New York: Basic Books.

Lincoln, Y. S. & Guba, E. G. (1985). *Naturalistic inquiry.* Beverly Hills, CA: Sage Publications.

Malinowski, B. (2002). *Argonauts of the Western Pacific; an account of native enterprise and adventure in the archipelagoes of Melanesian New Guinea.* London: Routledge.

Marcus, G. E. & Fischer, M. M. J. (1986). *Anthropology as cultural critique: An experimental moment in the human sciences.* Chicago: University of Chicago Press.

McLeod, J. (1987). *Ain't no makin' it.* Boulder, CO: Westview Press.

Mead, M. (1932). *The changing culture of an Indian tribe.* New York: Columbia University Press.

Mead, M. (1965). *Anthropologists and what they do.* New York: F. Watts.

Mead, M. (1973). *Coming of age in Samoa: A psychological study of primitive youth for Western civilization.* New York: Morrow Quill Paperbacks.

Miles, M. B. & Huberman, A. M. (1994). *An expanded sourcebook: Qualitative data analysis.* 2nd ed. Thousand Oaks, CA: Sage Publications.

Mishler, E. G. (1986). *Research interviewing: Context and narrative.* Cambridge, MA: Harvard University Press.

Merriam, S. B. (1998). *Qualitative research and case study applications in education.* San Francisco: Jossey-Bass.

Ogbu, J. U. (1974). *The next generation: An ethnography of education in an urban neighborhood.* New York: Academic Press.

Ogbu, J. U. (1978). *Minority education and caste: The American system in cross-cultural perspective.* New York: Academic Press.

Patton, M. Q. (1987). *How to use qualitative methods in evaluation.* Newbury Park, CA: Sage Publications.

Peshkin, A. (1986). *God's choice: The total world of a Christian fundamentalist school.* Chicago: University of Chicago Press.

Quantz, R. A. (1992). On critical ethnography (with some Postmodern considerations). In M. D. LeCompte, W. L. Millroy & J. Preissle (Eds.) *The handbook of qualitative research in education* (pp. 447–98). San Diego, CA: Harcourt Brace.

Radcliffe-Brown, A. R. (1965). *Structure and function in primitive society.* New York: Free Press.

Rist, R. C. (1973). *The urban school: A factory for failure—a study of education in American society.* Cambridge, MA: MIT Press.

Sanjek, R. (Ed.) (1990). *Fieldnotes: The making of Anthropology.* Ithaca, NY: Cornell University Press.

Schensul, J. J., LeCompte, M. D., Hess, G. A., Nastasi, B. K., Berg, M. J., Williamson, L., Brecher, J. & Glassert, R. (1999). *Using ethnographic data.* Vol. 7 in *The ethnographer's toolkit.* Walnut Creek, CA: AltaMira Press.

Schensul, J. J., LeCompte, M. D., Nastasi, B. K. & Borgatti, S. P. (1999). *Enhanced ethnographic methods.* Vol. 3 in *The ethnographer's toolkit.* Walnut Creek, CA: AltaMira Press.

Schensul, J. J., LeCompte, M. D., Trotter, R. T., Cromley, E. K. & Singer, M. (1999). *Mapping social networks, spatial data & hidden populations.* Vol. 4 in *The ethnographer's toolkit.* Walnut Creek, CA: AltaMira Press.

Schensul, S. L., Schensul, J. J. & LeCompte, M. D. (1999). *Essential ethnographic methods.* Vol. 2 in *The ethnographer's toolkit.* Walnut Creek, CA: AltaMira Press.

Spradley, J. P. (1980). *Participant observation.* Fort Worth, TX: Harcourt.

Strauss, A. & Corbin, J. (1990). *Basics of qualitative research: Grounded theory procedures and techniques.* Newbury Park: Sage Publications.

Turnbull, C. (1974). *The mountain people.* London: Pan Books.

VanMaanen, J. (1988). *Tales of the field: On writing ethnography.* Chicago: University of Chicago Press.

Willis, P. E. (1977). *Learning to labour: How working class kids get into working class jobs.* New York: Columbia University Press.

Wolcott, H. F. (1981). Home and away: Personal contrasts in ethnographic style. In D. A. Messerschmidt (Ed.) *Anthropologists at home in North America: Methods and issues in the study of one's own society.* New York: Cambridge University Press, 255-265.

Wolcott, H. F. (1994). *Transforming qualitative data: Description, analysis and interpretation.* Thousand Oaks, CA: Sage Publications.

Wolcott, H. F. (1999). *Ethnography: A way of seeing.* Walnut Creek, CA: AltaMira Press.

Wolcott, H. F. (2003). *The Man in the principal's office: An ethnography.* Walnut Creek, CA: AltaMira Press.

Wolcott, H. F. (2004). *The Art of fieldwork.* Walnut Creek, CA: AltaMira Press.

AWARD-WINNING CARTOONIST
SALLY CAMPBELL GALMAN IS
A PROFESSOR OF EDUCATION AT
THE UNIVERSITY OF MASSACHUSETTS.
SHE LIVES AND WORKS IN AMHERST,
MA WITH HER HUSBAND, BABY
AND CAT.